OVERCOMING BARRIERS

What Is Braille?

Deborah Kent

Enslow Elementary

an imprint of

Enslow Publishers, Inc.

40 Industrial Road
Box 398
Berkeley Heights, NJ 07922
USA

http://www.enslow.com

Enslow Elementary, an imprint of Enslow Publishers, Inc.
Enslow Elementary® is a registered trademark of Enslow Publishers, Inc.

Library of Congress Cataloging-in-Publication Data

Kent, Deborah.
    What is Braille? / Deborah Kent.
       p. cm. — (Overcoming barriers)
    Includes bibliographical references and index.
    Summary: "Discusses the history of Braille and how the blind community uses it in everyday life"—Provided by publisher.
    ISBN 978-0-7660-3770-0
    1. Braille—Juvenile literature. I. Title.
    HV1669.K46 2012
    411—dc22
                                2010038887

Future editions:
Paperback ISBN 978-1-4644-0155-8
ePUB ISBN 978-1-4645-1062-5
PDF ISBN 978-1-4646-1062-2

Printed in China

012012 Leo Paper Group, Heshan City, Guangdong, China

10 9 8 7 6 5 4 3 2 1

To Our Readers: We have done our best to make sure all Internet Addresses in this book were active and appropriate when we went to press. However, the author and the publisher have no control over and assume no liability for the material available on those Internet sites or on other Web sites they may link to. Any comments or suggestions can be sent by e-mail to comments@enslow.com or to the address on the back cover.

Contents

Kaitlyn and her family live on a farm. They raise animals, including goats.

Chapter 1

The Feel of the Words

Kaitlyn Ryan had two kindergarten teachers. One of them taught Kaitlyn and all the other children in her class. The other was Kaitlyn's Braille teacher. She spent time with Kaitlyn by herself each day. She taught Kaitlyn to read Braille with her fingers.

Kaitlyn was born blind. She does not read by looking at a book with her eyes. She reads by using her fingers. Braille is a touch-based way to read. It is used by blind people all over the world.

Today Kaitlyn is ten. She is starting fifth grade. She is now a good Braille reader. Most of her school books

Kaitlyn uses her Perkins Brailler machine to write.

are printed in Braille. She can read along with the rest of her class. They read the the words with their eyes. Kaitlyn glides her fingers over the lines on her Braille pages.

Braille also helps Kaitlyn write her work. Her Braille teacher copies her work in print. This way the classroom teacher can read it.

A teacher helps her student learn to use a special Braille writer.

This portable Braille computer helps blind people read what is on a computer screen.

Kaitlyn lives on a farm in Illinois. Her family raises corn, beans, beef cattle, and goats. Kaitlyn has raised several goats herself. She feeds and grooms them every day. One of her goats won first place in a statewide contest.

Kaitlyn loves to play outdoors. She likes to bounce on her trampoline and run around with her friends. On rainy days, however, she stays inside. Sometimes she reads or writes stories in Braille. Usually she uses a machine called a Perkins Brailler when she writes. She also has a Braille notetaker. The notetaker is like a computer with a Braille display instead of a screen. Kaitlyn knows that Braille is very useful and that it will help her throughout her life.

Let's read more about Braille and the people who use it.

Chapter 2

Sixty-Three Combinations

Take a look at the "6" on a domino. You will see two lines of dots side by side. Each line has three dots. The Braille code uses a set of six dots, called a cell. It is set up just like the domino "6."

Each dot in the Braille cell has a number. From top to bottom, the dots on the left side of the cell are numbered 1, 2, and 3. Dots 4, 5, and 6 are on the right side of the cell.

All of the letters of the Braille alphabet are formed by using certain dots within the cell. For instance, Dot 1 alone is the letter a. Dots 1 and 2 are the letter b, and

Braille Alphabet

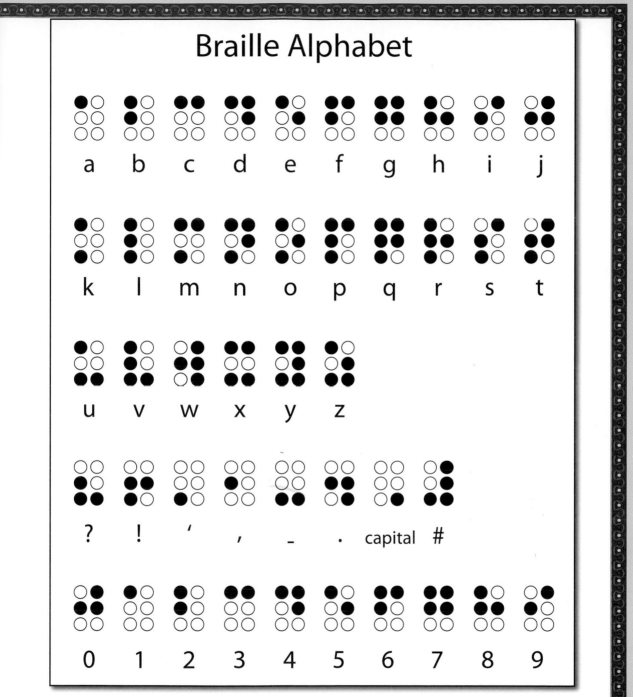

Each letter of the alphabet is created by using a different combination of dots.

Once people learn the Braille alphabet, they are on their way to reading books in Braille. This girl is reading one of the *Harry Potter* books.

the letter c is formed with Dots 1 and 4. A letter may contain one to five dots.

The Braille cell is also used to write all of the punctuation marks, such as the comma, period, question mark, and exclamation point. Numbers and musical notes can be written in Braille, too. Nearly anything that can be written in print can also be written in Braille. Altogether there are sixty-three possible combinations of the six dots in the Braille cell. Every one of them is used for something. Some combinations are used in several different ways.

Braille books are much bigger than print books. In fact, in Braille most books fill several large volumes. A Braille textbook, such as a math or science book, may come in ten or fifteen volumes, or even more. One book might fill an entire shelf in a bookcase.

To help save space, Braille uses many shortcuts. These shortcuts are called contractions. Some contractions stand for groups of letters that often occur together, such as ch, ou, ar, or ing. Some contractions are short ways of writing whole words. For instance, the letters gd stand for the word "good." Afn stands for "afternoon," and tm stands for "tomorrow." Altogether Standard English Braille uses more than four hundred contractions.

The Perkins Brailler machine (below) allows people to write in Braille faster than if they are using a slate and stylus (right).

Ways to Write Braille

There are several ways to write Braille. The Perkins Brailler is a machine with six keys. It has one key for each of the Braille dots. Letters are written by pressing the proper keys all at once. Braille can also be written by hand with a slate. A slate is a metal or plastic frame with rows of rectangular holes shaped like Braille cells. Letters are formed by punching dots with a pointed tool called a stylus. A Braille notetaker is a machine for writing Braille electronically. The machine's display has tiny metal pins that move up and down. The pins form the Braille letters.

The Royal Institute for
the Blind in Paris was
founded in 1786. It is
over 225 years old!

Chapter 3

Creating the Code

In 1821, French army captain Charles Barbier visited the Royal Institution for Blind Youth. Barbier had invented a way to read by touch. He called it "night writing." One night he had seen a tragedy take place. A soldier lit a lantern to read a message. The light showed the enemy where the soldier was hiding. He and his group were killed. Barbier invented night writing so that soldiers could read messages safely in the dark. He thought it also might be a way for blind people to read.

At that time books for the blind were written in raised print letters. Students learned to read the letters by touch, but reading was slow and difficult. Books in raised print were very scarce. The one hundred blind students at the Institution had only fourteen books.

Captain Barbier's writing system was very different from raised print. It was a code based on dots and dashes that stood for the letters of the alphabet. It was based on a cell containing twelve dots.

One student at the school, twelve-year-old Louis Braille, was very excited about Barbier's code. But Braille realized that the code was not perfect. There was no way to capitalize letters or to write punctuation. And words written in night writing did not use standard French spelling. But Louis Braille thought the code was a good start.

For the next three years, Louis worked on the code in every spare

Louis Braille created the Braille alphabet.

moment he had. He kept trying to make it better. When he was fifteen his writing system was complete. It was based on a cell of six dots that just fit beneath the tip of the reader's finger. The code included numbers, punctuation, and capitalization.

The boys at the institute loved Louis Braille's new writing system. As their hands slid across the lines of dots, the boys read smoothly and quickly. They asked sighted friends to read books out loud to them. The blind students copied the books word by word, using

Different Braille Reading Systems

By 1900, five reading systems for blind people were in use. Each system had a group of strong supporters. Boston Line Type and Moon Type were systems of raised lines based on print letters. New York Point and American Braille were reading systems that used dots. English Braille was Louis Braille's original code with the addition of many contractions.

Braille's writing system made it easier for blind students to read.

Louis Braille's code. Book by book, they began to build a library.

Many of the sighted teachers at the school did not like the new reading method. Because it was so different from print, they did not learn it easily. They said that using the new code would make blind people seem different from everyone else.

During the 1830s, the school director did not let the students use Braille's system. Any student who wrote notes in Braille's code was punished. Teachers even burned the books that Louis Braille and his friends had made.

No matter how hard the teachers tried to stop them, the students continued to use Braille's code. They kept it alive by teaching it to one another. Finally the director gave in. The Braille code, named in Louis Braille's honor, was approved by the school in 1843.

In 1860, the Missouri School for the Blind in St. Louis became the first school in the United States to use Braille. However, Braille was not yet widely accepted. More than a dozen other touch-based

Helen Keller

Helen Keller (1880–1968) was both deaf and blind. She spent her life working to improve the lives of blind people throughout the world. When she was in school she wanted to read all of the books she could find. She learned all five of the reading systems in use at the time.

Helen Keller became deaf and blind before her second birthday. She used sign language and Braille to learn and communicate.

reading systems were invented in the late 1800s. Most were used for only a short time.

Blind people and teachers of the blind knew that one way of reading was needed. But which one would be best? The struggle to pick a single reading system came to be known as the War of the Dots.

In 1932, English Braille was finally chosen as the standard writing system for the blind throughout the English-speaking world. Standard English Braille is used in the United States, the United Kingdom, Canada, and Australia. It is used in every country where English is spoken. The invention of Louis Braille, a blind teen in France, has brought the power of reading and writing to millions of people.

Forms of Braille are used for nearly every written language on earth. Each language has rules of its own. Most languages use their own contractions.

This woman works in an office and is transferring Braille to a computer.

Chapter 4

Braille at Work

When Louis Braille was growing up, few blind people held jobs. Today blind people work as teachers, lawyers, scientists, and engineers. They run businesses, take part in sports, and raise families.

Blind people who know Braille use it at school, at work, and at home. A blind dad reads to his children from books that have Braille and print on the pages. A blind teacher writes her lesson plans in Braille. A blind secretary uses Braille to keep track of phone numbers and meetings.

John Gwaltney learned Braille when he was a child. He used it to take notes when he was a student. He used it later as a college teacher. For a year he lived

Blind people can have lots of jobs. This man is a piano tuner.

in a mountain village in Mexico. Many people in the village were blind due to a disease carried by flies. Gwaltney's book *Thrice Shy* describes what he learned about the villagers and how they thought of the blind people among them.

Geerat Vermeij was born in the Netherlands. He moved with his family to the United States when he was three. His parents thought that the United States would offer the best opportunities for their blind son. Today Vermeij is one of the world's experts on sea shells. He studies shells from all of the world's oceans. Each shell in his large collection is labeled in Braille so he knows what it is and where it was found.

Geerat Vermeij became blind early in life. However, he has become one of the world's experts on sea shells.

Dionne Quan is a voice actress. She is the voice for different cartoon characters, including Kimi of the *Rugrats*.

Dionne Quan has always loved to read out loud. When she was growing up she created a variety of voices for the characters in her Braille books. At ten she began to take acting classes. When she was fourteen she got her first job, talking for a radio commercial. Quan became the voice of Kimi Finster, a character in the television series *Rugrats*. She has also played in other Nickelodeon shows, including *The Fairly OddParents* and *All Grown Up*. Quan reads her lines from a Braille script. Her voice goes out to millions of people.

Judy Redlich is the manager for group called Joni and Friends Gateway. This group runs programs for people with disabilities

Judy Redlich works on a Braille computer.

Sabriye Tenberken created Braille Without Borders so blind people around the world can learn to read Braille.

all over the world. Through its Wheels for the World Program, volunteers deliver wheelchairs to people in need in many different countries. Redlich leads teams to Mexico as part of this program. In 2009, she was named "Woman of the Year" in Media Relations by the National Association of Professional and Executive Women. Previously, Redlich helped build the Here's Help radio and TV network, hosted her own television show, and still hosts Internet radio shows. Most of her staff were people who were homeless. Redlich uses an electronic device with a Braille display for speaking presentations, appointments, and for reading when on the air.

As a blind teenager growing up in Germany, Sabriye Tenberken became fascinated with the faraway land of Tibet. When she found that there was no Braille code for the Tibetan language, she invented one herself. In 1997, Tenberken went to Tibet and started a school for blind children. She founded an organization called Braille Without Borders to promote the teaching and use of Braille around the world.

Screen Readers

Today most blind people use computers on the job, just as sighted people do. A program called a screen reader reads the words on the screen in a computerized voice. A blind person can also write in Braille on a notetaker. He can print out the file for people who do not know Braille.

A Braille computer helps blind people read what is on a computer screen.

Chapter 5

What Is the Future of Braille?

In 2009, people all over the world celebrated the 200th birthday of Louis Braille. An exhibit on the inventor's life and work was shown in the United States and Canada. Schools started Braille clubs and sponsored Braille reading contests. The United States issued a Louis Braille commemorative coin. More than forty countries printed Louis Braille stamps.

Louis Braille gave literacy to blind people. Literacy is the ability to read and write. For sighted people, literacy means knowing how to read and write in print.

Blind people use their hands to read braille

This girl is using her finger to read the Braille version of someone's name.

The ability to read and write Braille means literacy for blind people.

Some people worry that not enough blind children are learning Braille today. Only about 14 percent of blind children learn Braille. Many children who have poor vision only learn print, even though reading print is very hard for them. Braille could help them read more easily if they had the chance to learn.

Thousands of blind children do not read print or Braille. They mostly use recorded books. Recorded books are very helpful to blind people. However, they cannot take the place of Braille. By reading Braille, blind students learn how words are spelled. They learn where commas and periods belong in a sentence. Using Braille, a blind student can take notes in class. He or she can write papers for school or write stories for fun.

Braille is very useful for students learning math. By using Braille, a blind student can set up a math problem and work out the answer. It is much harder to grasp the layout of a problem by listening to an explanation.

Years ago a Braille transcriber had to copy each book word by word. Today computers turn print into Braille quickly and easily. Most digital files can be printed in Braille or read with a Braille notetaker.

Braille readers used to wait months or years to get a book that they wanted in Braille. Now they can choose from thousands of digital books on the Internet. A few hundred Braille books used to fill several rooms. Today a whole library can fit onto a memory stick.

Long ago in Paris, Louis Braille could not have guessed the future. The writing system he invented was simple and logical. Yet it has swept blind people into the age of computers.

This teen uses a Braille 'n Speak to help him understand the problems on his math test.

Mapping the World

Braille readers can learn geography by studying tactile maps. A tactile map is a map with raised lines and symbols. These raised maps show boundaries, rivers, cities, and other features. The places on a tactile map can be marked with Braille labels.

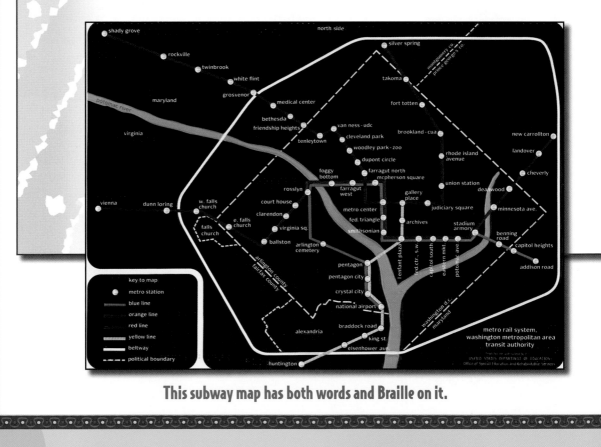

This subway map has both words and Braille on it.

A map with raised areas allows a blind person to understand what the world looks like and how states fit together.

To honor the 200th birthday of Louis Braille, the United States issued this silver dollar coin in 2009. You can feel the word "BRAILLE" on the coin.

Chapter 6

Looking Ahead

Kaitlyn Ryan is learning more about computers. She wants to learn to print out files she makes on her Braille notetaker. "I want to be able to print out my own work," she says. "Then I'll be able to turn it in without anyone having to translate the Braille for me." Kaitlyn loves living on the farm. "I think I'll always want to have a lot of animals," she says. "You know, dogs and cats and horses, and probably a lot of goats."

When she grows up, Kaitlyn would like to become a Braille teacher. "Braille is really important," she explains. "Blind kids need to learn it so they can keep

Kaitlyn Ryan uses a laptop computer.

up with everybody else. I think I'd have fun teaching Braille because I know it myself."

From her own life Kaitlyn knows the value of Braille. Someday she may share what she has learned. Perhaps she will teach other blind people so they too can enjoy the gift of literacy.

Words to Know

Braille display—An electronic device with metal pins that move up and down to form Braille letters.

Braille notetaker—An electronic device used for writing Braille and storing digital files to be read in Braille.

cell—A set of six dots in lines of three that is the basis for the Braille code.

contraction—A shortcut for writing a group of letters or a common word in Braille.

literacy—The ability to read and write.

Perkins Brailler—A machine with six keys used for writing Braille.

screen reader—A computer program that reads text on the screen in a computerized voice.

slate—A frame made of metal or plastic used for writing Braille by hand.

stylus—A pointed tool for punching Braille dots when using a slate.

transcriber—A person who translates books and other printed material into Braille.

Learn More

Books

Cottin, Menena. *The Black Book of Colors.* Toronto, Canada: Groundwood Books, 2008.

Donaldson, Madeline. *Louis Braille.* Minneapolis, Minn.: Lerner, 2007.

Smith, Kristie. *Dottie and Dots See Animal Spots: Learning Braille with Dots and Dottie.* Lincoln, Neb.: iUniverse, 2007.

Web Sites

Braille Bug.
<http://www.afb.org/braillebug>

How Braille Began.
<http://www.brailler.com/braillehx.htm>

You've Got Braille.
<http://www.pbskids.org/arthur/print/braille>

Index